THE CASE FOR
Easter

THE CASE FOR
Easter

*Investigating the Evidence
for the Resurrection*

STUDY GUIDE | 4 SESSIONS

LEE STROBEL

WITH BILL BUTTERWORTH

 ZONDERVAN®

Contents

How to Use This Guide

D o you have questions about the first Easter? Then you are in the right place. During the next four weeks, you and your group will look at the story surrounding the death and resurrection of Jesus—and how you can know the events recorded in the Bible are true.

The Case for Easter video study is designed to be experienced in a group setting such as a Bible study, Sunday school class, or any small group gathering. Each session begins with a brief introduction and opening questions to get you and your group thinking about the topic. You will then watch a video with Lee Strobel and jump into some directed small-group discussion. You will close each session with a time of prayer.

Each person in the group should have his or her own study guide, which includes video teaching notes, group discussion questions, and between-sessions personal studies to help you reflect on the material during the week. You are also encouraged to have a copy of *The Case for Easter* book, as reading it alongside the curriculum will provide you with deeper insights and make the journey more meaningful.

To get the most out of your group experience, keep the following points in mind. First, the real growth in this study will happen during your small-group time. This is where you will process the content of Lee's message, ask questions, and learn from others as you hear what God is doing in their lives. For this reason, it is important for you to be fully committed to the group and attend each session so you can build trust and rapport with the other members. If you choose to only "go through the motions," or if you refrain from participating, there is a lesser chance you will find what you're looking for during this study.

Second, the goal of your small group is to serve as a place where you can share, learn about God, and build intimacy and friendship with others. For this reason, seek to make your group a "safe place." This means being honest about your thoughts and feelings and listening carefully to everyone else's opinion. Resist the temptation to "fix" someone's problem or correct his or her theology, as that's not the purpose of your small-group time. Also, keep everything your group shares confidential. This will foster a rewarding sense of community in your group and create a place where people can heal, be challenged, and grow spiritually.

In between your group times, you can maximize the impact of the curriculum by completing the personal study activities. This individual study will help you reflect and actively respond to the lesson. You may wish to complete the personal study in one sitting or spread it over a few days (for example, working on it a half-hour per day on four different days that week). Note that if you are unable to finish (or even start!) your between-sessions personal study, you should still attend the group study video session. You are still wanted and welcome at the group even if you don't have your "homework" done.

Keep in mind that the videos, discussions, and activities are simply meant to kick-start your imagination so you will be open to what God wants you to hear through this study. The goal is for you to see the Easter story in a whole new light and know with confidence that the Gospel accounts of Jesus' death and resurrection are accurate and true. This will hopefully prove to be a journey that will stimulate your mind, warm your heart, and satisfy your soul.

Sound good? Then let's get started.

Note: If you are a group leader, there are additional resources provided in the back of this guide to help you lead your group members through the study.

Evidence for the Resurrection

. . . .

A man who was merely a man and said the sort of things Jesus said would not be a great moral teacher. He would either be a lunatic . . . or else he would be the Devil of Hell. You must make your choice. Either this man was, and is, the Son of God; or else a madman or something worse.

—C. S. Lewis, *Mere Christianity*

Introduction

For many of us, there were two stories in our childhood that captured the essence of Easter. Like the rails of a train track, the duo never intersected but ran in parallel tandem through our memories. The first was the story of the Easter Bunny. We heard tales of the happy white rabbit, dressed in human clothes, who would fill empty baskets with all sorts of our favorite chocolate candies . . . if we behaved ourselves throughout the year.

The other rail was more serious. It was the story of Jesus Christ, who died on the cross in a grotesque manner known as a *crucifixion* on Good Friday, but then miraculously rose from the grave on Easter Sunday to show his power over sin, death, and hell. Easter would likely find us dressed in our Sunday finest, attending a church service (whether we were regular church attenders or not), and returning home to baskets of melting chocolate while we waited for the family's traditional Easter dinner. If we were lucky, there would be an after-dinner Easter egg hunt featuring color-dyed, hard-boiled eggs.

The Easter Bunny and the resurrection of Jesus. One is decidedly childish, while the other represents the most profound event to ever occur in human history. But for many people today, believing Jesus' claims that he was the Son of God—and that he *actually* rose from the dead on the third day—is like believing the big magical bunny is real. They doubt whether the Gospel accounts can be trusted and prefer to pass off the story as a legend or mere mistake.

So, what proof do we have that Jesus' crucifixion and resurrection actually took place? How can we know that he actually was executed and died on a Roman cross those many years ago? And what does the reality of Jesus' resurrection mean in our lives? In this first session, we will start to dig into these issues by examining the events surrounding Good Friday and, in particular, the Roman execution-style murder that took place that day.

Before You Watch

Pair up with another group member, ideally someone you don't know that well, and briefly talk about the following questions:

- What was Easter like for you as a child? What was the best part for you? What was the worst part for you?
- What are some of your favorite Easter memories? How big a role did the resurrection of Jesus play in your typical Easter celebrations?
- Now that you are an adult, do you celebrate Easter any differently than you did as a child? What changes have you made in the way you celebrate?

Video Teaching

Play the video segment for session one. As you watch, use the following outline to record any thoughts or concepts that stand out to you.

Notes

Some have claimed there is no scriptural text in which Jesus said explicitly he was divine. But just because Jesus didn't make this claim directly doesn't mean he didn't make it at all.

Throughout the Gospels, Jesus' claims to divinity were crystal clear to his audiences—as if he had said outright, "I am God." For instance, in John 10:30, Jesus declared, "I and the Father are one," which caused his opponents to accuse him of blasphemy.

Christianity is an investigate-able religion. While the origins of many world religions are lost in the mists of history, Christianity makes specific claims about events that occurred in time and space—right there in the first century.

When we scrutinize the data of history, we find four facts that establish convincingly that Jesus rose from the dead—which we can call "the four *E*s." The first *E* stands for *execution*—Jesus was truly dead after being executed by the Romans at the behest of the Jewish leaders.

Before he was crucified, Jesus was flogged by Roman soldiers. In fact, he was evidently flogged *two separate times*. The Greek word used to describe the flogging indicates a punishment inflicted after a death sentence has been pronounced.

Because of the terrible effects of this beating, there's no question Jesus was already in serious-to-critical condition even before the nails were driven through his hands and feet.

Group Discussion

Once the video has concluded, break into small groups for a time of discussion. Ideally, the group should be no less than four people and no more than six. Don't be shy—grab your chair and circle up! Find someone who will become your partner over the next few weeks. If you're married and your spouse is in the group, you've got the option of choosing him or her, or you may opt for someone completely different. If not your spouse, it's best for women to choose another woman and men to choose another man. Get your new partner's cell phone number and email so you can connect during the week.

1. Do you have any doubts that Jesus clearly claimed that he was God? Are the statements covered in the video teaching evidence enough, or do you need further convincing? Be honest about your questions. That's why we're meeting!

2. Now that you've heard the teaching on the crucifixion of Jesus, did you find this type of execution was more painful and graphic than you previously believed? Why or why not?

3. What part of the execution of Jesus made the biggest impact on you as you heard it presented? Why do you think it affected you the way it did?

4. What other questions have you had about whether Jesus actually claimed to be God? What questions have you had about whether he really died on the cross—or even existed at all? How did this week's teaching help address these concerns?

Closing Prayer

Conclude your group discussion time with a few minutes for prayer. Share one another's needs and requests and offer them up to God. Nothing will bring your group together quicker than knowing you have brothers and sisters who care enough about issues you raise to bring them before the Lord for his answers and his direction.

SESSION 1

Between-Sessions Personal Study

Reflect on the content you've covered this week by engaging in any or all of the following between-sessions personal study. The time you invest will be well spent, so let God use it to draw you closer to him. At your next meeting, share with your group any key points or insights that stood out to you as you spent this time with the Lord.

Study God's Word

A good place to start our investigation into the resurrection is with Jesus' claims to be God. This week, examine Mark's account of Jesus' trial before the high priest. Note what Jesus says in this passage and how the high priest responds:

> The chief priests and the whole Sanhedrin were looking for evidence against Jesus so that they could put him to death, but

they did not find any. Many testified falsely against him, but their statements did not agree.

Then some stood up and gave this false testimony against him: "We heard him say, 'I will destroy this temple made with human hands and in three days will build another, not made with hands.'" Yet even then their testimony did not agree.

Then the high priest stood up before them and asked Jesus, "Are you not going to answer? What is this testimony that these men are bringing against you?" But Jesus remained silent and gave no answer.

Again the high priest asked him, "Are you the Messiah, the Son of the Blessed One?"

"I am," said Jesus. "And you will see the Son of Man sitting at the right hand of the Mighty One and coming on the clouds of heaven."

The high priest tore his clothes. "Why do we need any more witnesses?" he asked. "You have heard the blasphemy. What do you think?"

Mark 14:55–64

What stands out to you in this passage that you didn't notice previously?

One way to highlight and personalize the Scriptures is to use a technique called *paraphrasing*, where you rewrite the verses using your own words. By doing this, you can interact with the text in an intimate way. Take your time with this exercise. Start with a brief prayer, asking the Lord to help you as you work through the text. Next, take a few minutes to read through the entire passage again slowly and carefully. Then, begin your paraphrasing.

Write down a few statements to summarize how it felt to interact with the text in this way. Weave in some of this week's lessons along with the insights you are gleaning personally.

Put It into Practice

Take some time this week to think about how the material you are covering with your group can make a difference in the way you live your life. In the New Testament book of James, the author implores us to be *doers* of God's Word and not *hearers* only. The real test of what is important to us is how well we integrate it into our lives.

Can you put into a single sentence why it is important that Jesus makes unmistakable claims in the Gospels that he is God? Can you do the same for the execution of Jesus?

How does this week's lesson impact the way you would share your faith with someone else?

What is the biggest truth you learned this week? Write it down.

What are two more concepts that emerged from your study this week?

For many of us, coming to grips with the agony Jesus went through on our behalf is an emotional experience. The best way to deal with those emotions is to allow them to flow. Using the space provided on the next page, take a few minutes and compose a letter to Jesus, expressing what it means that he went through this for you and, most of all, *thanking him* for enduring it for your sake.

Dear Jesus:

Make contact with the partner you selected at the meeting either through a text or, better yet, a phone call. Check in to see how he or she is doing:

- Is the person enjoying the study? Why or why not?
- Is there any frustration or confusion that he or she can verbalize?
- How does trusting the Bible make a difference in the way that person is living his or her life?
- Is there anything you can do to be of help to them between now and the next time the entire group gets together?

Talk to your partner about the answers to the previous questions—the big truths you've come away with as a result of the study and how your time together has made an impact on you.

CLOSING REFLECTION

Even for a decorated cold-case homicide investigator, this was a formidable challenge. J. Warner Wallace had used his considerable detective skills to solve murders that were decades old, but he had never tackled a case that stretched back for two millennia.

What's more, this time he wasn't merely attempting to identify the perpetrator of a long-ago crime; instead, he was trying to determine whether the victim was truly deceased—and whether he defied all naturalistic explanations by rising from the dead three days later.

Quite an assignment for someone who was at the time a hyper-skeptical atheist....

I've always appreciated Wallace's no-nonsense "just-give-me-the-facts" exterior, which syncs up well with my own journalistic bent, but I also admire what's underneath—an exceedingly compassionate and gracious heart toward others. I know because I've been the grateful recipient of his kindness in the past.

Oddly, though, I had never talked at length with Wallace about his journey from atheism to faith. After we sat in his recreation room and chatted for a while about family, I asked, "What prompted you to start checking out the Gospels?"

"My wife Susie was raised with a cultural Catholicism, so she thought it was important to take the kids to church, and I went along," he explained. "One Sunday the pastor said, 'Jesus was the smartest guy who ever lived,' and our Western culture is grounded in his moral teaching."

"How did you react?"

"I thought, 'I'm a cop enforcing the penal code, but I know there's a universal moral law above that.' After all, adultery is legal, but it isn't right. So it got me thinking about where that moral code came from. That's why I went out and bought this."

He pulled a red pew Bible from the shelf and handed it to me. "I got this for six bucks," he said.

I flipped it open to a random page and saw that it was very neatly but quite thoroughly marked up. There were homemade tabs, notes in small print in the narrow margins, and color-coded underlining throughout. I went to the Gospel of Mark and saw that it was densely annotated.

"I was using forensic statement analysis to analyze the Gospels—for instance, here in the Gospel of Mark I was looking for the influence of Peter, so that's what one of the colors represents," he explained. "I was nitpicking the details; by the time I was done, I had gone through three Bibles."

"How long did your analysis take?"

"Six months."

"What was your verdict?"

"That the Gospels reliably recorded true events," he said. "But that presented a problem for me."

"Why?"

"Because they talk about the resurrection and other miracles," he said. "I could believe the Gospels if they said Jesus ate bread, but what if they said the loaf levitated? C'mon, I couldn't believe that. I didn't believe miracles could happen, so I rejected them out of hand."

I could relate to the impediment of the supernatural, since it was a stubborn obstruction in my own spiritual investigation. "What changed your mind?" I inquired.

"I asked myself, 'Do I believe anything supernatural?' And I concluded, that, well, yes, even as an atheist, I did believe something extra-natural occurred."

"For instance?"

"The Big Bang," he replied. "Everything came from nothing. If nature is defined as everything we see in our environment, then there had to be something before that, a first cause that was beyond space, matter, and time. That meant the cause couldn't be spatial, material, or temporal. . . . I realized that if there was something extra-natural that caused the beginning of all space, time, and matter as recorded in Genesis 1:1, then that same cause could accomplish all miracles recorded in the

Gospels. In other words, if there is a God, then miracles are reasonable, maybe even expected."

"So you got past your presupposition against the miraculous," I said.

"I did. As a detective, I knew presuppositions can derail an investigation. I remember a case in which a woman was found dead in her bed. She was a locally notorious drug addict, and there was drug paraphernalia on her nightstand. The patrol officers got there and didn't even bother to pull down the sheets, since this was so obviously an overdose. But when investigators got there, they pulled down the sheets—and they saw she had been stabbed to death."

He paused as the implications registered with me. "Presuppositions can be impediments to truth," he said. "The resurrection was the most reasonable inference from the evidence, but I was ruling out miracles from the outset."

"What led you to conclude that this first cause of the universe was personal and not just some force?"

"I recognized that there are universal moral laws," he replied. "For example, it's wrong to torture a baby for fun in any culture, anywhere, any time. And transcendent moral laws are more than simply truths—they are obligations between persons. If there are objective, transcendent moral obligations, the best explanation for them is an objective, transcendent moral person."

"Okay, you concluded the Gospels contain reliable eyewitness accounts, even of the miraculous," I said. "What came next?"

"I was stuck on the 'why' question: why did Jesus come, die, and return from the dead? I started analyzing Paul's writings, and I was amazed by his insights into what he called 'natural man' or sinful people. His description fit me in an uncanny way," he replied.

"Plus, the message of grace is so counterintuitive. Every other religion is based on performance, which makes sense because humans love to achieve and compete to get a reward. This message of grace—of unearned forgiveness—didn't sound like it had human origins. It came off as either ridiculous or divine. This doesn't prove anything in and of itself, but it was one more piece of the puzzle."

"In the end, then, it was a cumulative case," I said, a declaration more than a question.

"Bingo," he said crisply. "The totality of the evidence overwhelmed me. When we're trying to solve a homicide, we typically put all the facts on a white board and see if we can make the case. I didn't have to do that here. The case made itself."

—*Lee Strobel, from* The Case for Miracles

An Excruciating Execution

• • • • • • • •

Clearly, the weight of historical and medical evidence indicates that Jesus was dead before the wound to his side was inflicted.... Accordingly, interpretations based on the assumption that Jesus did not die on the cross appear to be at odds with modern medical knowledge.
—William D. Edwards, et al, "On the Physical Death of Jesus Christ"

Introduction

In 2012, the *Wall Street Journal* reviewed a newly written biography on our sixteenth president, Abraham Lincoln. In that review, a remarkable statistic was repeated. It was the answer to the question, "How many books have been written on Abraham Lincoln?" The answer?

More than 16,000.

That's a big number, wouldn't you agree? Of all these books, most scholars consider the most important writing to be that of two men who collaborated on a massive ten-volume work. Their names were John G. Nicolay and John Hay, and the reason for the significance of their work is that they were Lincoln's personal secretaries in the White House. Thus, their accounts of what transpired during Lincoln's life weren't based on stories passed down from others.

Being ten volumes in length, if you are courageous and patient enough to plow through all 4,700 pages, you will quickly realize the value of the work is that it captures the historical events of Lincoln's life from an immediate point of view. It also captures the details of his death. Writing about that fateful night when Lincoln was assassinated, the authors include specifics such as the fact that John Wilkes Booth had a gun in one hand and a knife in the other, that he leapt down to the stage but got caught on the flag hanging outside the box, and that when he stood up again with a broken leg, he shouted, *"Sic semper tyrannis!"*

One should not minimize the value of early accounts when attempting to reconstruct an event in history. The closer the sharing of the account is to the actual event, the more likely it is accurate and dependable. This principle doesn't just apply to Abraham Lincoln but is also true in relation to the resurrection of Jesus. We have early reports of what a Roman execution looked like in the first century—so we know for a fact that he actually died on the cross—and reports of his resurrection that came virtually right after his death.

In this session, we will dig deeper into some of those early reports to see what evidence they can provide that the Bible is accurate when it says that Jesus rose from the grave.

Before You Watch

Find someone you don't know that well in the group and talk about the following questions:

- Have you read a book about Abraham Lincoln or another famous person? Which one did you read? What were your impressions of it?
- If biographies aren't your cup of tea, what sort of reading do you like to do? If you were stuck on a desert island and could only have one book with you, what book would you choose? (*Shipbuilding for Dummies?*)
- How would you put into your own words the importance of early accounts of an event when attempting to reconstruct what actually happened?

Video Teaching

Play the video segment for session two. As you watch, use the following outline to record any thoughts or concepts that stand out to you.

Notes

For Jesus' crucifixion, we not only have multiple first-century accounts in the New Testament but also five sources outside the Bible: Josephus, a first-century Jewish historian; Tacitus, another early historian; Lucian; Mara Bar-Sarapion; and even the Jewish Talmud.

Several factors contributed to the cause of death in a crucifixion, including the great loss of blood, but primarily the cause of death was asphyxiation.

The first of the four *E*s is for *execution*—Jesus was dead. The second *E* stands for *early*. We have early reports that Jesus rose from the dead that came almost immediately after his death.

We have preserved for us a creed of the earliest church that says Jesus died, was buried, and rose on the third day, and it mentions specific individuals and groups to whom he appeared. This creed came too early to explain it away as being legendary.

The creed, recorded by Paul in 1 Corinthians 15, mentions at least 500 witnesses—most of whom were still living, though others had died. In a sense, Paul is saying, "If you don't believe me, go ask these eyewitnesses. They're still around. They'll confirm this story."

Right after Paul encountered the risen Jesus, he met with some apostles in Damascus. Many scholars believe it was *then* that Paul was given the creed; some say three years later. Either way, it means the beliefs that formed the creed go back virtually to the cross itself!

This creed mentions the risen Jesus appeared to James, who was not a follower during Jesus' lifetime. When James sees the evidence for the resurrection with his own eyes, he becomes a believer. What would it take to convince *you* that your brother was the Lord?

Group Discussion

Once the video has concluded, take a few minutes to catch up with your group members. If there are people new to your group, give them time to briefly introduce themselves. Then break up into small groups for a time of discussion. Ideally, this should be the group you formed during the last session, but you can create a new group of four to six people if necessary.

1. Why is it so important to know that we have early reports of the resurrection that came virtually right after the event?

2. Why is having such an early Christian "creed" important to the argument that Jesus rose from the dead? Are there specifics in that creed that lend greater significance to the argument for the empty tomb? Discuss these themes within your group.

3. Read aloud Matthew 27:32–44. What are some details in this passage that indicate it was based on early first-person accounts? Why are these significant?

4. What are some objections you have heard that the resurrection is not based on early and trustworthy accounts? How has this video teaching helped address these concerns? What other questions do you still have that you want to discuss with the group?

Closing Prayer

Conclude your group discussion time with a few minutes of prayer. Check in with everyone from last week in order to get updates on the requests for which group members are already praying. Then listen for other requests and bring them before the Lord.

Between-Sessions Personal Study

Reflect on the content you've covered this week by engaging in any or all of the following between-sessions personal study. The time you invest will be well spent, so let God use it to draw you closer to him. At your next meeting, share with your group any key points or insights that stood out to you as you spent this time with the Lord.

Study God's Word

As stated in this week's teaching, we have preserved for us a creed of the earliest church—a statement of conviction the first Christians rallied around, based on facts they knew to be true. This creed contains the essence of Christianity: it says Jesus died, was buried, rose on the third day, and appeared to specific individuals and groups. Read this creed on the next page, as recorded by the apostle Paul in his first letter to the Corinthians, and then circle any words that stand out to you.

Now, brothers and sisters, I want to remind you of the gospel I preached to you, which you received and on which you have taken your stand. By this gospel you are saved, if you hold firmly to the word I preached to you. Otherwise, you have believed in vain.

For what I received I passed on to you as of first importance: that Christ died for our sins according to the Scriptures, that he was buried, that he was raised on the third day according to the Scriptures, and that he appeared to Cephas, and then to the Twelve. After that, he appeared to more than five hundred of the brothers and sisters at the same time, most of whom are still living, though some have fallen asleep. Then he appeared to James, then to all the apostles, and last of all he appeared to me also, as to one abnormally born.

For I am the least of the apostles and do not even deserve to be called an apostle, because I persecuted the church of God. But by the grace of God I am what I am, and his grace to me was not without effect. No, I worked harder than all of them—yet not I, but the grace of God that was with me. Whether, then, it is I or they, this is what we preach, and this is what you believed.

But if it is preached that Christ has been raised from the dead, how can some of you say that there is no resurrection of the dead? If there is no resurrection of the dead, then not even Christ has been raised. And if Christ has not been raised, our preaching is useless and so is your faith. More than that, we are then found to be false witnesses about God, for we have testified about God that he raised Christ from the dead. But he did not raise him if in fact the dead are not raised. For if the dead are not raised, then Christ has not been raised either. And if Christ has not been raised, your faith is futile; you are still in your sins. Then those also who have fallen asleep in Christ are lost. If only for this life we have hope in Christ, we are of all people most to be pitied.

1 Corinthians 15:1–19

One way to look deeper into the meanings of the words in a passage is to read it in several different translations. Today, with the availability of translations on the internet, it's possible to read the Bible in many different versions. Pick two of your favorites, read the above passage again in those translations, and make note of key words that stand out to you.

Key Words from the Creed of the Earliest Church

New International Version:	Translation: _____	Translation: _____

Put It into Practice

Take some time this week to connect with your partner and discuss how the material you are covering can make a difference in the way you live your lives. What was the most significant takeaway your partner received in this last session? Share your most significant takeaway as well. If you sense any discouragement from your partner, do you best to cheer him or her on. Use the following questions to guide your discussion.

What difference does the empty tomb make in your life?

How does the fact that Jesus conquered the grave affect your outlook on life?

How are you extending the hope you have been given in Christ to other people?

In view of these truths, what can you do in the next forty-eight to seventy-two hours that will extend kindness and compassion to someone who really needs it? For example:

- Send an encouraging text or phone call to a friend or family member

- Take a meal to a homeless person
- Volunteer at the local Boys and Girls Club as a coach or a mentor
- Pay a visit to a senior adult at the local retirement center

Christ is alive in you, and you have the opportunity to demonstrate his love to a world that desperately needs him. Be brave. Be bold. Be creative. Ask God for help, and he will guide you.

CLOSING REFLECTION

Ah, the resurrection.

Even skeptics agree with the apostle Paul's assertion that if the resurrection were disproved, then the entire Christian faith would collapse into irrelevancy (see 1 Corinthians 15:17). Consequently, opponents are constantly minting fresh objections to undermine this central tenet of Christianity. In recent years, for example, agnostic New Testament scholar Bart Ehrman and others have advanced new efforts to cast doubt on whether Jesus died and escaped his grave alive again.

In my interview with J. Warner Wallace, I said, "Even if we concede that the gospel accounts are rooted in eyewitness testimony, we're still faced with the issue of whether a miracle the magnitude of the resurrection makes sense. Let me challenge you with some of the most potent objections to Jesus' rising from the dead."

"Shoot," he said, quickly catching himself with a chuckle. "Maybe that's not the best terminology for a cop. Anyway, yes, go ahead."

"It seems to me the two relevant issues are, first, whether Jesus was actually dead from crucifixion and, second, whether he was encountered alive afterward, necessitating an empty tomb," I said.

Wallace folded his arms. "Agreed," he replied.

"So how do we know he was really dead? Is it reasonable that he would succumb that soon? The thieves on either side of him were still alive."

"But the path to the cross for Jesus was dramatically different than the path for the thieves," he said.

"How so?"

"Pilate didn't want to crucify Jesus like the crowd was demanding, so he kind of makes an offer. He says, in effect, 'I'll tell you what I'll do—I'll beat him to within an inch of his life. Will that satisfy you?' Consequently, Jesus was given an especially horrific flogging. That didn't satisfy the crowds, and he was crucified. But he was already in such extremely bad shape that he couldn't even carry his cross."

"These soldiers weren't medical doctors," I said. "Maybe they thought Jesus had died when he hadn't."

"That objection usually comes from people who've never been around dead bodies. As a cop, I've witnessed a lot of autopsies. Let me tell you: dead people aren't like corpses in movies. They look different. They feel different. They get cold; they get rigid; their blood pools. These soldiers knew what death looked like; in fact, they were motivated to make sure he was deceased because they would be executed if a prisoner escaped alive. Plus, the apostle John unwittingly gave us a major clue."

"What's that?"

"He says when Jesus was stabbed with a spear to make sure he was dead, water and blood came out. In those days, nobody understood that. Some early church leaders thought this was a metaphor for baptism or something. Today, we know this is consistent with what we would expect, because the torture would have caused fluid to collect around his heart and lungs. So without even realizing it, John was giving us a corroborating detail."

I reached into my briefcase and removed a copy of the Qur'an, which I placed on the table between us. "Yet," I said, "there are more than a billion Muslims who don't believe Jesus was crucified. Many of them believe that God substituted Judas for Jesus on the cross."

Wallace picked up the Qur'an and paged through it. "Here's the problem," he said, handing it back to me. "This was written six hundred years after Jesus lived. Compare that to the first-century sources that are uniform in reporting that Jesus was dead. Not only do we have the gospel accounts, but we also have five ancient sources *outside* the Bible."

"Still, how can you disprove the claim that God supernaturally switched people on the cross?" I asked.

"That would mean Jesus was being deceptive when he appeared to people afterward. No, that would contradict what we know about his character. And how would you explain him showing the nail holes in his hands and the wound in his side to Thomas?"

"You have no doubt, then, that he was dead."

"No, I don't. When scholars Gary Habermas and Michael Licona surveyed all the scholarly literature on the resurrection going back thirty years, Jesus' death was among the facts that were virtually unanimously accepted," he said.

"Besides," he added, "crucifixion was humiliating—it's not something the early church would have invented. And we have no record of anyone ever surviving a full Roman crucifixion."

—*Lee Strobel, from* The Case for Miracles

The Case for the Empty Tomb

. . . .

Without the belief in the Resurrection, the Christian faith could not have come into being. The disciples would have remained crushed and defeated men. . . . The cross would have remained the sad and shameful end of [Jesus'] career. The origin of Christianity therefore hinges on the belief of the early disciples that God had raised Jesus from the dead.

–William Lane Craig, *The Son Rises*

Introduction

When is "empty" not really empty?

It's not a trick question. At face value, it would seem the common-sense answer would be *never*. Something is either without anything in it (empty) or with something in it (not empty). But there is a recent discovery that contradicts that logic.

"Empty" is not *really* empty . . . when you are referring to the gauge in your car that measures the amount of fuel left in your tank!

Several years ago, a group created a chart that identifies how much fuel a car typically has left when the gauge says *E* and the little light illuminates. The chart includes the fifty top selling cars in the United States. The least amount of gas in an "empty" fuel tank is in the Toyota Prius, which still has 1.6 gallons remaining. The greatest amount of "empty" is in the tank of a GMC Sierra Denali or a Toyota Tundra, which has around 4 gallons remaining.

Translated, when your car's gas gauge says the tank is empty, you still have between 25 and 114 miles left to get to the nearest gas station. Thus, empty is not really empty.

When it comes to the resurrection of Jesus, people today often take the same approach. The tomb in which Jesus was laid wasn't *really* empty because he was never put there in the first place. Or Jesus' body was moved, and people only thought the tomb was empty. Or the disciples just made up the whole story. For these people, it's all just word play.

But for followers of Christ, the story we find in the Gospels doesn't give us that option. Either Jesus rose from dead . . . or he didn't. It's either an empty tomb . . . or he was still in there. In this session, we will explore what the evidence has to say about Jesus truly rising again.

Before You Watch

Find someone you don't know that well in the group and discuss the following questions:

- Do you have a story or two about times when you've run out of gas? Pick the best one and share it.
- How low do you tend to let your car's gas gauge go before you fill up the tank? Do you typically "run on fumes" before filling up or do you gas up sooner?
- Do you agree that when it comes to the resurrection, the tomb was either empty or it wasn't—no middle ground, no elaborate plots, no undercover scams? Why or why not?

Video Teaching

Play the video segment for session three. As you watch, use the following outline to record any thoughts or concepts that stand out to you.

Notes

Some skeptics say the reason the tomb was empty was because Jesus' body was never put in it in the first place. However, the Gospel accounts are consistent with archaeological evidence and with Jewish practices of law.

A summary of Roman practice and procedure of the time, known as the *Digesta,* states "the bodies of those who are condemned to death should not be refused their relatives . . . [they] should be given to whoever requests them for the purpose of burial."

There are three lines of evidence that converge to make a case for the vacant tomb:

> The Jerusalem factor: The site of Jesus' tomb was known to everyone. If it were not empty, it's unlikely the Christian movement would have been founded.

> The criterion of embarrassment: If you felt the freedom to make up a lie, you would never include something that damaged your own cause.

Enemy attestation: The opponents never said Jesus was still in the tomb—they said the disciples stole the body. They conceded the tomb was vacant.

We can draw great comfort from the fact Jesus conquered the grave, because it means we will too, if we follow him. At times when life seems fragile, that's a wonderful encouragement!

Group Discussion

Once the video has concluded, break up into small groups for a time of discussion. Ideally, this should be the group with whom you've spent the previous two sessions—and by now you should be more comfortable with one another. Grab your chair and circle up!

1. If the location of the tomb was well known in both the Christian and the non-Christian community, why would the followers of Jesus set out to perpetrate a lie surrounding it? How does this lend weight to the fact the tomb was really empty?

2. How does the fact that all the Gospels state women discovered the tomb to be empty lend credibility to it being true?

3. What does the fact that the opponents of Jesus never asked the disciples to *prove* the tomb was empty say about what they were conceding? How does this enemy attestation support the argument that the resurrection was true?

4. How has this week's teaching helped you to answer any questions you've had in the past about whether Jesus' tomb was really empty? What would you now say to someone who claimed Jesus' body was never entombed, or was moved, or that the followers of Jesus just made up the story?

Closing Prayer

Close your time together with prayer. By now your group has most likely bonded over a few of the requests that have been mentioned, so get a brief follow-up on the items for which you've been praying. Gather any new requests and talk to the Lord together as a group.

Between-Sessions
Personal Study

Reflect on the content you've covered this week by engaging in any or all of the following between-sessions personal study. The time you invest will be well spent, so let God use it to draw you closer to him. At your next meeting, share with your group any key points or insights that stood out to you as you spent this time with the Lord.

Study God's Word

One of the clearest narratives on the resurrection of Jesus is found in Matthew's Gospel. Not only are we told the events, but Matthew clearly identifies people who observed the empty tomb as part of the story. Read this passage carefully, and while reading, circle the characters who are mentioned in the account:

> After the Sabbath, at dawn on the first day of the week, Mary Magdalene and the other Mary went to look at the tomb.

There was a violent earthquake, for an angel of the Lord came down from heaven and, going to the tomb, rolled back the stone and sat on it. His appearance was like lightning, and his clothes were white as snow. The guards were so afraid of him that they shook and became like dead men.

The angel said to the women, "Do not be afraid, for I know that you are looking for Jesus, who was crucified. He is not here; he has risen, just as he said. Come and see the place where he lay. Then go quickly and tell his disciples: 'He has risen from the dead and is going ahead of you into Galilee. There you will see him.' Now I have told you."

So the women hurried away from the tomb, afraid yet filled with joy, and ran to tell his disciples. Suddenly Jesus met them. "Greetings," he said. They came to him, clasped his feet and worshiped him. Then Jesus said to them, "Do not be afraid. Go and tell my brothers to go to Galilee; there they will see me."

While the women were on their way, some of the guards went into the city and reported to the chief priests everything that had happened. When the chief priests had met with the elders and devised a plan, they gave the soldiers a large sum of money, telling them, "You are to say, 'His disciples came during the night and stole him away while we were asleep.' If this report gets to the governor, we will satisfy him and keep you out of trouble." So the soldiers took the money and did as they were instructed. And this story has been widely circulated among the Jews to this very day.

Then the eleven disciples went to Galilee, to the mountain where Jesus had told them to go. When they saw him, they worshiped him; but some doubted. Then Jesus came to them and said, "All authority in heaven and on earth has been given to me. Therefore go and make disciples of all nations, baptizing them in the name of the Father and of the Son and of the Holy

Spirit, and teaching them to obey everything I have commanded you. And surely I am with you always, to the very end of the age."

Matthew 28:1–20

Check the items you circled to see if they match the names listed in the table below. In the right-hand column, write a summation of what is said about that individual, specifically how it relates to the empty tomb. (Note that some will have a more significant role than others.)

Character	Significance to the Story
Mary Magdalene	
The "other Mary"	
Angel of the Lord	
Guards	
Jesus	

cont.

Character	Significance to the Story
Chief priests	
Eleven disciples	

Each of the characters mentioned in this passage—some of whom were Jesus' followers and some of whom were his opponents—show there were firsthand reports of the empty tomb. Today, offer up a prayer of thanks to God for his Word and for helping you to achieve a better understanding of this text.

Put It into Practice

In the previous session, you examined the evidence for Jesus' execution. In this session, you focused on the empty tomb—his resurrection. It's now time to take what you have learned and put together a defense for the resurrection of Jesus. Think of this as an "elevator speech," meaning you have only three minutes to make your case. What would you say in that short period of time? Use the following prompts to chart out your presentation. Write it up in outline form, or word for word, or with bullet points, or whatever is most helpful to you.

Here is how I would make the case that Jesus claimed to be God . . .

Here is how I would make the case that Jesus actually died . . .

Here is how I would make the case that Jesus rose again . . .

Now that you've created this presentation, is there someone you would like to share it with? Who in your world wrestles with this foundational concept of the Christian faith? Is there a way you could reach out to this person with the good news—a visit, a call, a letter, an email? Spend some time reflecting on this idea and see if the Lord puts someone specific on your heart. Then, in obedience, follow his guidance and reach out.

CLOSING REFLECTION

Even the skeptical Bart Ehrman concedes that Jesus was killed by crucifixion, but he recently wrote a book (*How Jesus Became God*) saying it's "unlikely" that Jesus was buried in a tomb, saying that "what *normally* happened to a criminal's body is that it was left to decompose and serve as food for scavenging animals." . . .

Ironically, one of Ehrman's own colleagues at the University of North Carolina at Chapel Hill, a Jewish archaeologist named Jodi Magness, affirmed (in *Where Christianity Was Born*), "The Gospel accounts describing Jesus' removal from the cross and burial are consistent with archaeological evidence and with Jewish law."

Whatever occurred nearly two thousand years ago, there's little dispute that the disciples *believed* the once-dead Jesus appeared to them alive. Not only do the four Gospels report this, but there's confirmation from students of the apostles (Clement and Polycarp), as well as in an early creed of the church found in 1 Corinthians 15:3–8 and a speech by Peter in Acts 2.

"You've broken a lot of conspiracy cases as a cop," I said to J. Warner Wallace. "Do you see any way these people could have been lying about this?"

"For a conspiracy to succeed, you need the smallest number of coconspirators; holding the lie for the shortest period of time; with excellent communication between them so they can make sure their stories line up; with close familial relationships, if possible; and with little or no pressure applied to those who are telling the lie. Those criteria don't fit the resurrection witnesses.

"On top of that," he added, "they had no motive to be deceitful. In fact, we have at least seven ancient sources that tell us the disciples were willing to suffer and even die for their conviction that they encountered the risen Jesus."

"But," I interjected, "research has shown that history is murky on what actually happened to some of them."

"True, but what's important is their *willingness* to die. That's well established. They knew the truth about what occurred, and my experience is that people aren't willing to suffer or die for what they know is a lie.

"Even more importantly, there isn't a single ancient document or claim in which any of the eyewitnesses ever recanted their statement. Think about that for a minute. We have ancient accounts in which second-, third-, or fourth-generation Christians were forced to recant, but *no* record of an eyewitness ever disavowing their testimony. I think that helps establish the truthfulness of the eyewitnesses."

I tried another approach. "I'm sure you've seen cases where people close to a murder victim are so full of grief that it colors their recollections about what happened," I said.

"To some degree," he replied. "But I sense where you're going with this: Did the sorrow of the disciples cause them to have a vision of the risen Jesus? That's a different matter altogether."

"Why?"

"First, groups don't have hallucinations, and the earliest report of the resurrection said five hundred people saw him. Second, Jesus was encountered on numerous occasions and by a number of different groups. The vision theory doesn't seem likely in those varying circumstances. And I can think of at least one person who *wasn't* inclined toward a vision."

"Paul?"

"Yeah, he was as skeptical as, well, Michael Shermer."

"What if one of the disciples—maybe Peter—experienced a vision due to his sorrow and then convinced the others that Jesus had returned? As you know, Peter had a strong personality and could be persuasive."

"I've had murder cases where one emphatic witness persuaded others that something happened," Wallace conceded. "Inevitably, the persuader has all the details in their most robust form, while the others tend to generalize because they didn't actually see the event for themselves. But this theory can't account for the numerous, divergent, and separate group sightings of Jesus, which are described with a lot of specificity. Also, Peter wasn't the first to see the risen Jesus."

"Good point," I said.

"I'll add one last point," said Wallace. "With all these theories of visions or hallucinations, the body is still in the tomb."

I asked Wallace, "What happened when you finally concluded that none of the escape hatches would let you avoid the conclusion that the resurrection really happened?"

"I remember being in church one Sunday, though I can't recall what the pastor was saying," he said. "I leaned over and whispered to Susie that I was a believer." . . .

"It sounds like a cliché," Wallace continued, "but coming to faith in Christ changed me drastically over time. As someone forgiven much, I learned to forgive others. After receiving God's grace, I was better able to show compassion. Now my life is consumed with letting others know that faith in Christ isn't just a subjective emotion, but it's grounded in the truth of the resurrection."

I thought of the words of the apostle Paul, himself a hardened law enforcer who was transformed after encountering the risen Jesus: "Therefore, if anyone is in Christ, the new creation has come: The old has gone, the new is here!" (2 Corinthians 5:17).

—*Lee Strobel, from* The Case for Miracles

Eyewitnesses to the Resurrection

· · · · · · · ·

If Jesus rose from the dead, then you have to accept all that he said; if he didn't rise from the dead, then why worry about any of what he said? The issue on which everything hangs is not whether or not you like his teaching but whether or not he rose from the dead.

Timothy Keller, *The Reason for God*

Introduction

Some of us are old enough to recall a long weekend in November of 1963. President John F. Kennedy had traveled to Dallas, a city that had not been all that warm and accepting of him in previous months. The hope was that he could shake some hands, press the flesh, and win over these proud Texans with his charm, wit, grace . . . and his lovely first lady.

Air Force One landed without incident at Love Field, and the Kennedys got into their Lincoln Continental convertible. After driving a bit, they rounded the turn into Dealey Plaza—and you know the rest of the story. The president was victim to an assassin's bullet.

Later, the culprit, Lee Harvey Oswald, was apprehended at a local movie theater and charged with the crime. By now, the press was ubiquitous in the downtown area. It seemed like every move made by the police or the lawyers or the politicians was thoroughly covered by the large band of journalists.

So it's not surprising that when Lee Harvey Oswald was brought out of his holding cell to be transported to another location, the press smothered the movement like a blanket on a humid night. All who watched were eyewitnesses to the stunning scene that happened next. Jack Ruby moved into the crowd and fired his pistol, shooting Oswald in the midsection. The events happened quickly, but they would be played and replayed thousands of times because of the cameras that captured it for the ages.

Think for a minute about those two shootings. The public witnessed Kennedy being shot in his limousine, but they certainly didn't see who the killer was. No one had their camera locked on the Texas School Book Depository. But not only did the public see Oswald murdered, but they also saw the man who did it.

The camera doesn't lie. We were all eyewitnesses to the crime. In the same way, all of us know the facts surrounding the resurrection of Jesus, but we have further evidence available to us. We have a "snapshot" of the events through the word of eyewitnesses—men and women who saw the empty tomb with their own eyes and reported what they found. In this final session, we will see how these firsthand accounts can help us make the case for Easter.

Before You Watch

Find someone you don't know that well in the group and talk about the following questions:

- If you're old enough to recall, share where you were when you first heard of JFK being shot. If that's too old school for you, share where you were when you heard about the 9/11 attacks on the World Trade Center.
- Have you ever been called to a courtroom trial to testify on what you saw during the committing of a crime? Share what it was like for you to experience that role as a witness.
- Why are eyewitnesses important to the account of the empty tomb?

Video Teaching

Play the video segment for session four. As you watch, use the following outline to record any thoughts or concepts that stand out to you.

Notes

We have no fewer than nine ancient sources, both inside and outside the New Testament, to support the conviction of the disciples that they had encountered the resurrected Jesus.

The first source is the creed from 1 Corinthians 15. This comes quickly after Jesus' death, and was apparently given to Paul by two witnesses named in the creed—Peter and James.

The second source is Paul's testimony about the disciples. Paul interacted with some of the disciples and reported they were stating Jesus had risen from the tomb.

The third source is the book of Acts written by Luke. Even skeptical historians concede the book of Acts contains the teaching of the apostles through its summaries of their sermons.

The next four sources for the disciples being eyewitnesses to the resurrection are Matthew, Mark, Luke, and John. We've seen how these Gospels pass the tests of historicity.

The eighth source is Clement. Clement was an early leader who conversed personally with the apostles and confirmed them proclaiming the message of Jesus' resurrection.

The ninth source is Polycarp. Polycarp was instructed by the apostles and verified they were proclaiming "him who died for our benefit and for our sake was raised by God."

Jesus' resurrection isn't a legend, mythology, make-believe, a fairy tale, or wishful thinking. Rather, it is a historical reality, and that has implications for our lives.

Group Discussion

Once the video has concluded, break up into small groups for a final time of discussion. Once again, try to get with the same people you have been meeting with for the past sessions.

1. As you peruse the list of nine sources confirming the disciples were eyewitnesses to the resurrection, which one, in your opinion, offers the most compelling argument? Why?

2. Have someone in the group reread aloud the creed of the early church found in 1 Corinthians 15:1–11, perhaps this time in a different translation. What strikes you as you hear the words of the apostle Paul testifying to the truth of the resurrection?

3. We have terrorists today who are willing to die for their faith because they believe they will go to heaven as a result. What is the difference between this and the disciples' willingness to die for their faith by proclaiming the message of Jesus' resurrection?

4. What has this four-week study meant to you? What are two or three things you've learned as a result of our time together? For what questions did you get answers? What questions are still rolling around in your mind as unanswered?

Closing Prayer

Take a few moments for one final session of prayer. Thank the Lord for the answers he has delivered to your group during the past few weeks and continue to approach him for the ones that continue to be mentioned. If appropriate, share your contact information with other group members so you can remain connected even after this study has concluded.

Final Personal Study

Reflect on the content you've covered this final week by engaging in any or all of the following personal study. Think about what you've learned during this study and how it has strengthened your faith in the story of Jesus' death and resurrection as told in the Gospels. The time you invest in this last time of study will be well spent, so let God use it to draw you closer to him.

Study God's Word

During this week's teaching, you looked at nine sources from within and outside the New Testament that affirm the disciples were proclaiming that Jesus had risen from the dead. Carefully consider the following passages from Acts:

> When he [Paul] came to Jerusalem, he tried to join the disciples, but they were all afraid of him, not believing that he really was a disciple. But Barnabas took him and brought him to the apostles. He told them how Saul on his journey had seen the Lord and

that the Lord had spoken to him, and how in Damascus he had preached fearlessly in the name of Jesus.

Acts 9:26–27

"Fellow Israelites, listen to this: Jesus of Nazareth was a man accredited by God to you by miracles, wonders and signs, which God did among you through him, as you yourselves know. This man was handed over to you by God's deliberate plan and foreknowledge; and you, with the help of wicked men, put him to death by nailing him to the cross. But God raised him from the dead, freeing him from the agony of death, because it was impossible for death to keep its hold on him."

Acts 2:22–24

"Now when David had served God's purpose in his own generation, he fell asleep; he was buried with his ancestors and his body decayed. But the one whom God raised from the dead did not see decay."

Acts 13:36–37

Which of the nine witnesses would each reference fall under?

Acts 9:26–27

Acts 2:22–24

Acts 13:36–37

Circle the key words in each passage. Why do you consider those words important?

Look up a biography of Clement and Polycarp on the internet. As you read their biographies, list two or three significant statements that stand out from the life of each of these men.

Clement
    1.
    2.
    3.

Polycarp
    1.
    2.
    3.

Put It into Practice

A good way to incorporate the nine sources that support the conviction the disciples encountered the resurrected Jesus is to write them out for yourself. Look at the notes you took during this week's teaching and fill in the blanks in the chart on the next two pages:

Source	Reference	What This Says About the Apostles' Claims
Early Creed	1 Corinthians 15:3–8	
Paul's testimony	1 Corinthians 15:9–11	
Sermons in Acts	Acts 2:14–40 Acts 13:16–41	
Gospel of Matthew	Matthew 28:1–20	
Gospel of Mark	Mark 16:1–20	
Gospel of Luke	Luke 24:1–53	
Gospel of John	John 20:1–29	

cont.

Source	Reference	What This Says About the Apostles' Claims
Clement	Letter to the Corinthians	
Polycarp	Letter to the Philippians	

Now that you've covered the four *E*s in connection with the resurrection of Jesus, this would be a perfect time to share what you've learned with someone else. Choose a person who might be called a "seeker"—someone who does not have a relationship with Christ but is open to the truth—and talk with him or her. It just might be the four *E*s that win the person to Christ! Share "the truth in love" (Ephesians 4:15)—with tact and grace.

CLOSING REFLECTION

As someone who covered criminal justice as a journalist for years, I'm fascinated by how DNA evidence has been used to solve crimes that happened decades earlier. For J. Warner Wallace, though, DNA hasn't been a factor in any cold case he has solved.

"Typically, we've solved them through the analysis of eyewitness testimony," he said. "And that's the way I tested the Gospels."

"Michael Shermer believes they're just moral stories that don't have a historical core to them," I said. "Why are you convinced they're based on eyewitness accounts?"

"There's good evidence that John and Matthew wrote their Gospels based on their eyewitness testimony as disciples of Jesus. While Luke wasn't a witness himself, he said he 'carefully investigated everything from the beginning' (Luke 1:3), presumably by interviewing eyewitnesses. According to Papias, who was the bishop of Hierapolis, Mark was the scribe of the apostle Peter—and my forensic analysis of Mark's Gospel bears that out."

"In what ways?"

"Mark treats Peter with the utmost respect and includes details that can best be attributed to Peter," Wallace replied. "Mark also makes a disproportionate number of references to Peter. And unlike the other Gospels, Mark's first and last mention of a disciple is Peter, which is an ancient bookending technique where a piece of history is attributed to a particular eyewitness.

"Of course," he continued, "Peter called himself an eyewitness (see 1 Peter 5:1; 2 Peter 1:16–17), and John said he was reporting what 'we have seen with our eyes' (1 John 1:1). In fact, when they were arrested for testifying about the resurrection, they said, 'We cannot help speaking about what we have seen and heard' (Acts 4:20). Over and over, the apostles identified themselves as 'witnesses of everything he [Jesus] did in the country of the Jews and in Jerusalem'" (Acts 10:39).

"Nevertheless," I interjected, "you and I both know that eyewitness testimony has been challenged in recent years.

In fact, some defendants convicted by eyewitness testimony have been exonerated through new DNA evidence."

"No question—all eyewitness accounts have to be tested for reliability. In California, judges give jurors more than a dozen factors to weigh in evaluating an eyewitness account," he said. "We can apply these tests to the Gospels—for instance, is there any corroboration, did the witnesses have a motive to lie, did their stories change over time? When we do, we find they hold up well." . . .

"But what about the conflicts among the various Gospel accounts—don't they cast doubt on the reliability of the eyewitness testimony?" I asked.

"Based on my years as a detective, I would expect the four Gospels to have variances," he replied. "Think of this: the early believers could have destroyed all but one of the Gospels in order to eliminate any differences between them. But they didn't. Why? Because they knew the Gospels were true and that they told the story from different perspectives, emphasizing different things."

"The conflicts aren't evidence they were lying?"

"People might assume that if they've never worked with eyewitnesses before. In my experience, eyewitness accounts can be reliable despite discrepancies. Besides, if they meshed too perfectly, it would be evidence of collusion."

That echoed the assessment of Simon Greenleaf of Harvard Law School, one of America's most important legal figures, after he studied the Gospels. "There is enough of discrepancy to show that there could have been no previous concert among them," he wrote (in *The Testimony of the Evangelists*), "and at the same time such substantial agreement as to show that they all were independent narrators of the same great transaction."

Interestingly, I was recently reading a breakthrough book by New Testament scholar Michael R. Licona (*Why Are There Differences in the Gospels?*), published by Oxford University Press, which offers one innovative way to resolve differences between the Gospels. Licona, who earned his doctorate at the University of Pretoria, is a noted resurrection scholar and a colleague of mine at Houston Baptist University.

His research shows that many apparent discrepancies between the Gospels can be explained by the standard compositional techniques that Greco-Roman biographers typically used in that era. As Craig Keener pointed out in my interview with him for this book, the Gospels fall into the genre of ancient biography.

For example, one common technique, modeled by the historian Plutarch, is called "literary spotlighting." Licona likened this to a theatrical performance where there are multiple actors on stage but the lights go out and a spotlight shines on only one of them.

"You know other actors are on the stage," he said, "but you can't see them because the spotlight is focused on one person."

Applying this to the Gospels, he noted that Matthew, Mark, and Luke say multiple women visited Jesus' tomb and discovered it empty. However, John's Gospel only mentions Mary Magdalene. Is that a discrepancy that casts doubt on the Gospels?

"It seems likely that John is aware of the presence of other women while shining his spotlight on Mary," Licona said. "After all, he reports Mary announcing to Peter and the Beloved Disciple, 'They have taken the Lord from the tomb and we don't know where they have laid him' (see John 20:2). Who's the 'we' to whom Mary refers? Probably the other women who were present.

"Then observe what happens next," Licona continued. "In John, Peter and the Beloved Disciple run to the tomb and discover it empty, whereas Luke 24:12 mentions Peter running to the tomb and no mention is made of the beloved disciple. However, just twelve verses later, Luke reports there were more than one who had made the trip to the tomb (see Luke 24:24). These observations strongly suggest Luke and John were employing literary spotlighting in their resurrection narratives."

Based on exhaustive analysis of the Gospels, Licona reaches this conclusion: "If what I'm suggesting is correct—that an overwhelming number of Gospel differences are . . . most plausibly accounted for by reading the Gospels in view of their biographical genre—*the tensions resulting from nearly all of the differences disappear.*"

Consequently, he said, the argument that the Gospels are historically unreliable due to their differences would be "no longer sustainable."

—Lee Strobel, from The Case for Miracles

Leader's Guide

Thank you for your willingness to lead your group through this study! What you have chosen to do is valuable and will make a great difference in the lives of others. The rewards of being a leader are different from those who are participating, and we hope that as you lead you will find your own walk with Jesus deepened by this experience.

The Case for Easter is a four-session study built around video content and small-group interaction. As the group leader, think of yourself as the host. Your job is to take care of your guests by managing the behind-the-scenes details so that when everyone arrives, they can enjoy their time together. As the leader, your role is not to answer all the questions or reteach the content—the video, book, and study guide will do that work. Your job is to guide the experience and cultivate your small group into a kind of teaching community. This will make it a place for members to process, question, and reflect—not receive more instruction.

Before your first meeting, make sure everyone in the group gets a copy of the study guide. This will keep everyone on the same page and help the process run more smoothly. If some group members are unable to purchase the guide, arrange it so that people can share the resource with other group members. Giving everyone access to all the material will position this study to be as rewarding an experience as possible. Everyone should feel free to write in his or her study guide and bring it to group every week.

Setting Up the Group

You will need to determine with your group how long you want to meet each week so you can plan your time accordingly. Generally, most groups like to meet from one to two hours, so you could use one of the following schedules:

Section	60 minutes	90 minutes	120 minutes
INTRODUCTION (members arrive)	5 minutes	5 minutes	10 minutes
BEFORE YOU WATCH (discuss the icebreaker questions as directed)	10 minutes	15 minutes	15 minutes
VIDEO TEACHING (watch the video teaching material together and take notes)	15 minutes	15 minutes	15 minutes
GROUP DISCUSSION (discuss the Bible study questions you selected)	25 minutes	40 minutes	60 minutes
CLOSING PRAYER (reflect on the takeaways, pray together, and dismiss)	5 minutes	15 minutes	20 minutes

As the group leader, you will want to create an environment that encourages sharing and learning. A church sanctuary or formal classroom may not be as ideal as a living room, because those locations can feel formal and less intimate. No matter what setting you choose, provide enough comfortable seating for everyone, and, if possible, arrange the seats in a semicircle so everyone can see the video easily. This will make transition between the video and group conversation more efficient and natural.

Also, try to get to the meeting site early so you can greet participants as they arrive. Simple refreshments create a welcoming atmosphere and can be a wonderful addition to a group study evening. Try to take food and pet allergies into account to make your guests as comfortable as possible. You may also want to consider offering childcare to couples with children who want to attend. Finally, be sure your media technology is working properly. Managing these details up front will make the rest of your group experience flow smoothly and provide a welcoming space in which to engage the content of *The Case for Easter*.

Starting the Group Time

Once everyone has arrived, it is time to begin the group. Here are some simple tips to make your group time healthy, enjoyable, and effective.

Begin the meeting with a short prayer and remind the group members to put their phones on silent. This is a way to make sure you can all be present with one another and with God. Next, facilitate the "Before You Watch" icebreaker questions, using the directions provided in the study guide. This won't require as much time in session one, but beginning in session two, you may need more time if people also want to share any insights from their personal studies.

Leading the Discussion Time

Now that the group is engaged, watch the video and respond with some directed small-group discussion. Encourage the group members to participate in the discussion, but make sure they know they don't have to do so. As the discussion progresses, follow up with comments such as, "Tell me more about that," or, "Why did you answer that way?" This will allow the group participants to deepen their reflections and invite meaningful sharing in a nonthreatening way.

Although there are only four discussion questions for each session, you do not have to use them all or even follow them in order. Feel free to pick and choose questions based on either the needs of your group or how the conversation is flowing. Also, don't be afraid of silence. Offering a question and allowing up to thirty seconds of silence is okay. It allows people space to think about how they want to respond and also gives them time to do so.

As group leader, you are the boundary keeper for your group. Do not let anyone (yourself included) dominate the group time. Keep an eye out for group members who might be tempted to "attack" folks they disagree with or try to "fix" those having struggles. These kinds of behaviors can derail a group's momentum, so they need to be steered in a different direction. Model active listening and encourage everyone in your group to do the same. This will make your group time a safe space and create a positive community.

The group discussion leads to a closing time of reflection and prayer. During this time, encourage the participants to review what they have learned and share any needs they have with the group. Close your time by taking a few minutes to pray for those needs and to thank God for the gift of life he offers through the resurrection of his Son. The group members may also want to share requests they want the other members to pray about during the week. Beginning in session two, be sure to check in regarding these requests and see how God has answered them.

At the end of each session, invite the group members to complete the between-sessions personal study for that week. If you so choose, explain you will provide some time before the video teaching next week for anyone to share insights. Let them know sharing is optional, and it's not a problem if they can't get to the between-sessions activities some weeks. It will still be beneficial for them to hear from the other participants and learn about what they discovered.

Thank you again for taking the time to lead your group. You are making a difference in the lives of others and having an impact on the kingdom of God.

The Case for Easter

A Journalist Investigates the Evidence for the Resurrection

Lee Strobel
New York Times Bestselling Author

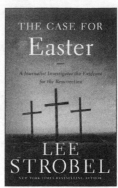

Did Jesus of Nazareth really rise from the dead?

Of the many world religions, only one claims that its founder returned from the grave. The resurrection of Jesus Christ is the very cornerstone of Christianity.

But a dead man coming back to life? In our sophisticated age, when myth has given way to science, who can take such a claim seriously? Some argue that Jesus never died on the cross. Conflicting accounts make the empty tomb seem suspect.

How credible is the evidence for—and against—the resurrection? Focusing his award-winning skills as a legal journalist on history's most compelling enigma, Lee Strobel retraces the startling findings that led him from atheism to belief. He examines:

- The Medical Evidence—Was Jesus' death a sham and his resurrection a hoax?
- The Evidence of the Missing Body—Was Jesus' body really absent from his tomb?
- The Evidence of Appearances—Was Jesus seen alive after his death on the cross?

Written in a hard-hitting journalistic style, *The Case for Easter* probes the core issues of the resurrection. Jesus Christ, risen from the dead: superstitious myth or life-changing reality? The evidence is in. The verdict is up to you.

Available in stores and online!

The Case for Christmas

A Journalist Investigates the Identity of the Child in the Manger

Lee Strobel
New York Times Bestselling Author

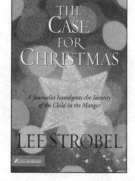

Who was in the manger that first Christmas morning? Some say he would become a great moral leader. Others, a social critic. Still others view Jesus as a profound philosopher, a rabbi, a feminist, a prophet, and more. Many are convinced he was the divine Son of God.

Who was he—really? And how can you know for sure?

Consulting experts on the Bible, archaeology, and messianic prophecy, Lee Strobel searches out the true identity of the child in the manger. Join him as he asks the tough, pointed questions you'd expect from an award-winning legal journalist. If Jesus really was God in the flesh, then there ought to be credible evidence, including:

- Eyewitness Evidence—Can the biographies of Jesus be trusted?
- Scientific Evidence—What does archaeology reveal?
- Profile Evidence—Did Jesus fulfill the attributes of God?
- Fingerprint Evidence—Did Jesus uniquely match the identity of the Messiah?

The Case for Christmas invites you to consider why Christmas matters in the first place. Somewhere beyond the traditions of the holiday lies the truth. You will find this little book a timely product, perfect as a gift or for use in ministry during the Christmas season or any other time of the year.

Available in stores and online!

The Case for Miracles

A Journalist Investigates Evidence for the Supernatural

Lee Strobel
New York Times Bestselling Author

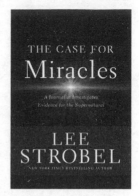

New York Times bestselling author Lee Strobel trains his investigative sights on the hot-button issue of whether it's credible to believe God intervenes supernaturally in people's lives today.

This provocative book starts with an unlikely interview in which America's foremost skeptic builds a seemingly persuasive case *against* the miraculous. But then Strobel travels the country to quiz scholars to see whether they can offer solid answers to atheist objections. Along the way, he encounters astounding accounts of healings and other phenomena that simply cannot be explained away by naturalistic causes. The book features the results of exclusive new scientific polling that shows miracle accounts are much more common than people think.

What's more, Strobel delves into the most controversial question of all: what about miracles that *don't* happen? If God *can* intervene in the world, why doesn't he do it more often to relieve suffering? Many American Christians are embarrassed by the supernatural, not wanting to look odd or extreme to their neighbors. Yet, *The Case for Miracles* shows not only that the miraculous is possible but that God still does intervene in our world in awe-inspiring ways. Here's a unique book that examines all sides of this issue and comes away with a passionate defense for God's divine action in lives today.

Available in stores and online!

The Case for Christ

A Journalist's Personal Investigation of the Evidence for Jesus

Lee Strobel
New York Times Bestselling Author

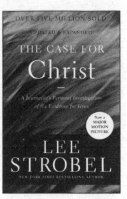

Is there credible evidence that Jesus of Nazareth really is the Son of God?

Retracing his own spiritual journey from atheism to faith, Lee Strobel, former legal editor of the *Chicago Tribune*, cross-examines a dozen experts with doctorates from schools like Cambridge, Princeton, and Brandeis who are recognized authorities in their own fields.

Strobel challenges them with questions like: How reliable is the New Testament? Does evidence for Jesus exist outside the Bible? Is there any reason to believe the resurrection was an actual event?

Winner of the Gold Medallion Book Award and twice nominated for the Christian Book of the Year Award, Strobel's tough, point-blank questions read like a captivating, fast-paced novel. But it's not fiction. It's a riveting quest for the truth about history's most compelling figure.

The new edition includes scores of revisions and additions, including updated material on archaeological and manuscript discoveries, fresh recommendations for further study, and an interview with the author, who tells dramatic stories about the book's impact, provides behind-the-scenes information, and responds to critiques of the book by skeptics. As *The Case for Christ* and its ancillary resources approach 10 million copies in print, this updated edition will prove even more valuable to contemporary readers.

Video Curriculum Also Available!

Available in stores and online!

In Defense of Jesus

Investigating Attacks on the Identity of Christ

Lee Strobel
New York Times Bestselling Author

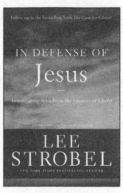

Has modern scholarship debunked the traditional Christ? Has the church suppressed the truth about Jesus to advance its own agenda? What if the real Jesus is far different from the atoning Savior worshiped through the centuries?

In Defense of Jesus, the follow-up to the bestselling *The Case for Christ* by Lee Strobel, explores such hot-button questions as:

- Did the church suppress ancient non-biblical documents that paint a more accurate picture of Jesus than the four Gospels?
- Did the church distort the truth about Jesus by tampering with early New Testament texts?
- Do new insights and explanations disprove the resurrection?
- Have fresh arguments disqualified Jesus from being the Messiah?
- Did Christianity steal its core ideas from earlier mythology?

Evaluate the arguments and evidence being advanced by prominent atheists, liberal theologians, Muslim scholars, and others. Sift through expert testimony. Then reach your own verdict with *In Defense of Jesus*.

Available in stores and online!

ZONDERVAN®